THE
CONGRESS

AMERICA'S LAWMAKERS

Gary M. Stern

A Blackbirch Graphics Book

RSVP
RAINTREE
STECK-VAUGHN
PUBLISHERS

Austin, Texas

© Copyright 1993 Steck-Vaughn Company

All rights reserved. No part of the material protected by this copyright may be reproduced or utilized in any form or by any means, electronic or mechanical, including photocopying, recording, or by any information storage and retrieval system, without permission in writing from the copyright owner. Requests for permission to make copies of any part of the work should be mailed to:
Copyright Permissions, Steck-Vaughn Company
P.O. Box 26015, Austin, TX 78755

A Blackbirch Graphics Book

Printed and bound in Mexico

1 2 3 4 5 6 7 8 9 0   RRD   98 97 96 95 94 93

Library of Congress Cataloging-in-Publication Data

Stern, Gary M..
    The Congress: America's lawmakers/ written by Gary M. Stern
        p.   cm.— (Good citizenship library)
    Includes bibliographical references (p.   ) and index.
    Summary: Discusses the origins of Congress, the members of Congress, how Congress works, and notable debates and acts of Congress.
    ISBN 0-8114-7351-1   ISBN 0-8114-5579-3 (softcover)
    1. United States. Congress—History—Juvenile literature.
2. Legislators—United States—History—Juvenile literature. [1. United States. Congress—History. 2. Legislators—History.] I. Title II. Series.
JK1064.S75 1992
328.73'09—dc20
                                              92-27030
                                                  CIP
                                                      AC

Acknowledgments and Photo Credits

Cover: © Wm. Clark, National Park Service, U.S. Dept. of Interior; p. 4: Blackbirch Graphics, Inc.; pp. 7, 8: North Wind Picture Archives; pp. 10, 13, 19: National Portrait Gallery, Smithsonian Institution; p. 14: Smithsonian Institution; pp. 17, 43: Collections of the Library of Congress; pp. 25, 26: AP/Wide World Photos; p. 29: © Jim Bourg/Gamma Liaison; pp. 39, 44: © Terry Ashe/Gamma Liaison; p. 40: Bettman; p. 45: © Markel/Gamma Liaison.
Charts by Sandra Burr.

Photo research by Grace How

Contents

The Origins

of Congress

 Eleven-year-old Michelle was watching a news report on television about an upcoming election for senator in her state. That night at the dinner table she said, "Ma, who are you voting for next week in the big election?" Her mother replied, "I'm too busy to vote. I have to work and take care of the house and you. It doesn't matter anyway. Politics doesn't affect us much."

Michelle's teacher, Mrs. Ramirez, was starting a unit on the United States Congress. Mrs. Ramirez told the class that they would study Congress, its history, and its influence on all citizens. She said that Congress was very important and affected all of our lives. Michelle wondered what influence Congress

Opposite:
The Capitol Building in Washington, D.C., houses the chambers where the members of the House of Representatives and the Senate meet.

5

had on both her life and her mother's or on her neighborhood and her school. She wanted to know more so she could convince her mother to vote.

Michelle began to read the newspaper. She noticed many articles mentioning Congress. Congress passed laws on taxes, unemployment programs, air pollution, and other issues. How did a law get passed? How did Congress develop? If Congress affected our lives so much, why did her mother pay so little attention to it?

What Is Congress?

The United States Congress is one of the three branches of our government. It is called the "legislative" branch because it has the power to make and pass laws. The other two divisions are the "executive" and the "judicial" branches. The executive branch, which is headed by our nation's president, has the right to reject laws that Congress wants to pass. The United States Supreme Court, the most powerful body in the judicial branch, can declare a law unfair according to our Constitution. But only Congress can make our laws.

Congress consists of two parts: the House of Representatives and the Senate. Each has different powers and responsibilities. Both work to create the laws that affect our lives. How much are we taxed? How much money should go to our defense budget, education budget, or to building highways and bridges? Should we have a new law to protect the civil rights of citizens? Should disabled people have special rights? Should students from poor families receive special scholarships for college?

Citizens of the United States elect members of the House and the Senate. These congressional members—100 in the Senate and 435 in the House of Representatives—represent the 260 million people who live in America in the 1990s. As the people's representatives, Congress is one of the solid foundations of our democracy, which is a government by the people. Members of Congress decide on the laws that govern our nation. Because we the people elect those members, we influence what our laws will be.

British Roots

To understand how Congress developed, one must start with the British, who ruled in America until the American Revolution in 1776. Over the course of English history, a body called Parliament had evolved. It had two parts, the House of Lords and the House of Commons. The House of Lords was made up of men from the landowning aristocracy (lords, or peers), whose membership was passed down for generations from father to son, and certain high churchmen. The members of the House of Commons were elected by property owners in the towns. Parliament was originally supposed to advise the king, or monarch, in governing the country, but gradually came to have more and more power.

Colonial Assemblies

The English started to settle America in the early 1600s. In 1607, a British trading company brought an adventurous group of men to America and created Jamestown (Virginia), the first permanent colony. Plymouth (Massachusetts) was founded next, in 1620. Soon British colonies were forming all along the eastern coast of America.

The various settlements soon began to develop governments that resembled that of England. A governor, who was appointed by the king, a trading company, or in a few cases an Englishman who had been given the right to found a colony, was assisted

Some of America's earliest governments were formed by Pilgrim settlers who landed in North America in the early 1600s.

and advised by an elected group of lawmakers called an assembly. The earliest assembly formed was the Virginia House of Burgesses, which held its first formal meeting in 1619.

All citizens were not allowed to vote in colonial America. The colonies followed England's example and granted only property owners the right to vote. In some colonies, one had to own at least 25 acres to vote. Women, children, and blacks were not allowed to vote even if they owned property.

The assemblies, like Parliament, possessed two important powers: (1) voting on taxes and how the money was spent, and (2) developing legislation. Because they controlled the colonial purse strings, assemblies could make decisions about the military, Indian relations, tax collection, and printing. Their power began to grow. It exceeded, in many ways, that of the Parliament in England. Self-government became a way of life for the settlers in each of the 13 colonies.

The colonies remained happily separate from each other and loyal to England until the 1700s. In fact, the first time several colonies united to achieve a common goal was prompted by Great Britain. The increasing presence of French traders in America was posing the first serious threat to Britain's desire to colonize the land for itself. The French had even started to build forts in certain areas, threatening British control. In 1754, battles erupted between French and American soldiers.

Benjamin Franklin drafted a document in 1754, called the Plan of Union. It proposed a government headed by a chief executive and an assembly of 48 members.

Hearing about the battles in America, the English Board of Trade urged a meeting of representatives from the colonies in Albany in 1754.

The Albany Congress, as it was called, is best remembered for supporting the Plan of Union. Written by Benjamin Franklin, the plan called for a chief executive, a powerful governor to be called the President-General of the United Colonies, and an assembly called the Grand Council, with 48 members chosen by the colonial assemblies. This council would oversee defense and relations with Native Americans, and would establish taxes to pay for its programs. The colonies did not adopt the Albany Plan. But it did lead Great Britain to name a supreme commander for British forces in America.

The Struggle with Britain

The English defeated the French in America in the French and Indian War, which lasted from 1754–1763. But winning the war created a major problem for the British government. It had gone into debt to pay for the long war. Also, it wanted to keep a permanent British army in North America. Where would it turn to raise the needed funds?

Great Britain decided to turn to its American settlers, believing that they should help pay for the war. For the first time, Parliament taxed the colonies to raise money, not just to regulate trade. It had placed earlier taxes on such products as molasses, liquor, and sugar. In 1764, Parliament passed a new law, commonly called the Sugar Act, that extended the existing taxes and imposed more taxes on foreign textiles, wines, and coffee. Still another law, the Stamp Act of 1765, taxed all papers—leases, newspapers, pamphlets, and insurance policies.

Many American colonists thought that the British government was trying to take advantage of them. Colonists began to hear and read a now-famous American slogan—"No taxation without representation"—in speeches and pamphlets. Many colonists believed that since they had no vote in Britain's Parliament, Parliament had no right to tell them what to do and no right to tax them. The colonists began to organize themselves in protest.

For several years after the Stamp Act, Parliament would impose taxes or pass other unpopular laws, the colonists would protest, and Parliament would retreat. During this period, the various American colonies learned to work together. Together, they decided not to purchase British goods. Colonial assemblies began to speak out against taxes and laws that they considered unfair.

Relations between Britain and the colonies went rapidly downhill in 1773. In that year Parliament passed a new act governing the shipping of tea to the colonies. The law imposed only a small tax on tea. But it favored the British East India Company, helping it to compete unfairly against merchants in the colonies. In 1773, the outraged citizens of Boston dumped a shipment of East India Company

King George III of England angered American colonists by taxing them unfairly.

tea into the waters of Boston Harbor—an event known to history as the Boston Tea Party. Then other seaport towns followed Boston's example.

Parliament responded with the Coercive Acts, laws that were meant to coerce, or force, the colonies to do what Parliament told them. The colonists called the new laws the Intolerable Acts, and responded with stronger protests.

Members of the Virginia assembly soon met and proposed a "Continental Congress," which would include representatives from all the existing colonies. Assemblies in New York, Pennsylvania, and Rhode Island were also requesting a meeting of all the colonies. George Washington urged colonists to hold such a meeting, saying that they must either assert their rights or be slaves of Britain.

The Continental Congress

On September 5, 1774, the First Continental Congress met in Philadelphia. It was made up of 56 elected members and a secretary. The members represented 12 of the colonies and would vote by colonies. The Congress's goal was to issue a series of protest papers and resolutions.

The Continental Congress passed resolutions declaring the Intolerable Acts to be unlawful and calling for boycotts against all British businesses. Showing their fighting spirit, the delegates to the Continental Congress rejected Parliament's right to control the colonies' affairs. They resolved that the

colonial assemblies should have the right to make their own laws concerning taxation and their internal affairs. They also condemned Britain's decision to keep a standing army in colonial towns during peacetime.

The conflict between Britain's rule of the colonies and the colonists' desire for greater self-government soon turned violent. In 1775, British soldiers received secret orders to prevent the frustrated colonists from rebelling. In Concord, Massachusetts, British soldiers started destroying American property and even shooting at colonists. The colonial militia returned the fire, and the American Revolution began.

By the time the Second Continental Congress met on May 10, 1775, the colonies were in turmoil.

The Second Continental Congress met in 1775, just before the first major battle of the Revolution.

It was the Declaration of Independence, written by Thomas Jefferson in 1776, that formally announced to Britain that America would govern itself in the future.

On the next day, Fort Ticonderoga in upstate New York was seized from the British. Colonial soldiers in Boston were also fighting British forces. The Continental Congress began to act more like a government. It quickly named George Washington commander-in-chief of its forces. It also decided to print paper money to fund the war.

On June 17, 1775, the first major battle of the Revolution began at Bunker Hill near Boston. Still, the Congress tried to reach a compromise with the British to stop the war. It issued the Olive Branch Petition, announcing its loyalty to the king, and urged a resolution to the conflict. The angry king refused even to read the Olive Branch Petition.

Despite the battles that were breaking out, many colonists were still not sure about engaging Britain in a war. In his famous pamphlet *Common Sense,* Thomas Paine convinced many fellow colonists that independence was a sensible option. One by one, the colonies passed resolutions that the United Colonies should be independent

In CONGRESS, July 4, 1776.

The unanimous Declaration of the thirteen united States of America.

of Britain. On July 2, 1776, the Continental Congress voted for independence. On July 4, 1776, it passed Thomas Jefferson's Declaration of Independence, which said governments should receive their power from the people and announced America's right to declare itself free of British rule.

But Britain was unwilling to give up the colonies without a fight. Soon American soldiers were battling British soldiers all through the colonies.

Congress Under the Articles of Confederation

As the Revolutionary War raged, the Continental Congress drafted the Articles of Confederation in 1781. They established a new central government for the former colonies. But reacting to their battles with the king, the newly proclaimed states decided to limit the powers of their own government. The Articles called for a government without a president and without a central court. The Confederation Congress could not tax the states or regulate interstate or foreign commerce. Nine of the 13 states had to approve any measure dealing with war.

Despite their weaknesses, the Articles of Confederation set down principles for a federal government. And they reinforced the central role a congress would play in that government. The Articles granted Congress several powers, including responsibility for foreign affairs, war and peace, and settling disputes between states; authority over currency, postal service, and Native American affairs; and authority over the western territories.

The Articles governed the states all through the Revolution, and for some years afterward. But many people were unhappy with the weaknesses of the Articles of Confederation. Finally, in 1787, state leaders met and called a convention to revise the Articles. Fifty-five delegates, most chosen by their state's conventions, attended the Constitutional Convention. Thirty-nine of them eventually signed the Constitution. The delegates came from various occupations; they included lawyers, merchants, bankers, and farmers. George Washington served as presiding officer; 81-year-old Benjamin Franklin added his experience. James Madison, a Virginia lawyer, was a chief writer of the Constitution.

The Constitution Is Created

Two founding principles of the Constitution were that governments must serve the people and that people must be protected from the possibility of losing their rights and freedoms. The Constitution created a system of checks and balances so no one branch of government would have too much power.

Unlike events in the present, which are captured by the media, much of the discussion and debate about the Constitution was conducted in private. If James Madison had not taken extensive notes during the meetings, we might never have known how the Constitution was created.

The Virginia and New Jersey Plans

The Virginia Plan was presented by Edmund Randolph, the governor of the state. It was a proposal for writing a new constitution, instead of revising the Articles of Confederation. The plan proposed a truly national government that would be made up of three separate branches: legislative, executive, and judicial. The legislative, or "law-making," branch would be the congress. The executive branch would carry out, or "execute" the laws and would be headed by a president. The judicial branch would consist of courts that would settle disputes about the laws and punish people who broke them; it would be headed by a national supreme court.

George Washington headed the Constitutional Convention of 1787. The purpose of the meeting was to revise the Articles of Confederation.

Under this plan the congress would have two houses. In both houses the states would be represented according to their size. That is, the states with larger populations would have more representatives in both houses. The lower house would be elected by the people. Delegates to the lower house would then elect the upper house.

Not everyone liked the Virginia Plan. The states with smaller populations were especially upset by the idea that a state's representation in both houses would be based on its population.

William Paterson, a delegate from New Jersey, offered another proposal called the New Jersey Plan. This plan would only rework the Articles of Confederation, not create an entirely new government. All the states would have the same number of votes in the congress, but the new congress would have some of the powers that the Confederation Congress had lacked. It would be able to tax and make rules about trade; it would appoint a group of persons to act as an executive branch; and it would appoint a supreme court. Most important, the Congress's acts and any treaties it agreed to would have to be followed, even if a state law said something different.

The Great Compromise

The most populated and least populated states disagreed over the two plans. The states with the most people favored the Virginia Plan because it based representation on population. Delegates from the states with fewer people preferred the New Jersey Plan because it allowed one vote for each state regardless of population. Finally, Roger Sherman of Connecticut proposed a solution. It came to be called the "Great Compromise." Like all good compromises, it gave both groups what they wanted. Under Sherman's plan, the number of delegates to one of the houses of congress, the "House of Representatives," would be determined by population. But in the other house, called "the Senate," each state would have two delegates, called "senators," regardless of its population.

The Federal System of Government

In the discussions about what kind of government the United States should have, people were divided about whether the states or the central government should have more power. Some people thought that the states were more important, and that any national government should above all be an association of strong state governments. Others thought that this was one country and one people, and that the states should obey a strong central government.

Another question about which there was much discussion was how much power the people should have and how much power the government should have over them. The Revolution had been fought to secure the colonists' rights against the king and

Roger Sherman was responsible for the "Great Compromise" at the 1787 Constitutional Convention.

Parliament. America's Founders, the people who wrote the Constitution, believed in basic human ·rights, individual freedom, and justice for all. They also believed that laws could secure these rights. But some people feared that governments were always trying to take away those rights. They believed that the less government a nation had, the safer people's rights would be.

Others believed in a strong government. They argued that ordinary citizens might not be wise enough to choose good leaders, and that the majority might trample on other people's rights, if it were given too much power. They also believed that a government with too little power might not do what needed to be done for the welfare of the United States. (Too little power had been one of the problems with the Articles of Confederation.)

Through their debates, the Founders created a compromise. To deal with the question of state versus national power, they created a federal system. This type of government amounted to two systems —a central government and state governments. A citizen was responsible to both the state he or she lived in and the United States. The states yielded many of their powers to the central government. For example, the central government was ultimately responsible for military defense, foreign affairs, and coinage. But the Constitution said that any power not expressly given to the central government remained with the states.

Three Branches of the Federal Government

To deal with the fears of tyranny (too powerful a government) versus anarchy (no government at all or mob rule), America's Founders created a system of "checks and balances." The central government's three branches would each act as a check on the power of the others.

The Branches of Government

EXECUTIVE

The President

- Symbol of our nation and head of state
- Shapes and conducts foreign policy and acts as chief diplomat
- Chief administrator of the federal government
- Commander-in-chief of armed forces
- Authority to pass or veto congressional bills, plans, and programs
- Appoints and removes non-elected officials
- Leader of his or her political party

LEGISLATIVE

The Congress:
The Senate
The House of Representatives

- Chief lawmaking body
- Conducts investigations into matters of national importance
- Has power to impeach or remove any civil officer from office, including the president
- Can amend the Constitution
- The Senate is made up of 100 senators— 2 from each state
- The House of Representatives is made up of 435 congressional representatives, apportioned to each state according to population

JUDICIAL

The Supreme Court

- Protects the Constitution
- Enforces commands of the executive and legislative branches
- Protects the rights of individuals and shields citizens from unfair laws
- Can declare laws unconstitutional
- Defines the laws of our nation

As set forth in the Constitution, there were several ways that each branch could keep the others from being too powerful. Congress could pass a bill, but the president could veto, or reject, that bill; but then, if two-thirds of the members of Congress agreed, they could pass the bill over the president's veto. The president would be commander-in-chief of the armed forces, but only Congress could declare war. The president could negotiate treaties with foreign countries, but the Senate had to approve them by a two-thirds vote. The president could appoint judges and diplomats, but the Senate had to approve them, too. Finally, if Congress believed the president had committed treason, bribery, or another serious crime, it could accuse and try him. The president would appoint judges with the approval of the Senate, and Supreme Court judges would serve for life.

Also, although it was not clearly given the power in the Constitution, the Supreme Court has come to have the right to declare acts of Congress or the executive branch unconstitutional. Thus, if the Congress or a state passes a law that conflicts with the Constitution, the Supreme Court can say that the law need not be followed.

By 1790, the 13 states had voted to accept the Constitution. Congress had replaced the colonial assemblies, and the Constitution became the law of the land. Today, this document remains the basis for all the new laws—both old and new—that we live by.

Powers Given to Congress

The most important role of the United States Congress is to make laws. Only Congress can make laws concerning taxes and borrowing money. Only Congress can declare war. Only Congress can make laws about national defense. However, Congress cannot make any laws that disagree in any way with the Constitution. If such laws are made, the Supreme Court can reject those laws. Congress can change the Constitution; that is called an amendment. For an amendment to pass, two-thirds of the states must agree to it.

Although the president is commander-in-chief of the armed forces, Congress also helps provide for the defense of the country. It funds the armed forces and plays a major role in running the Army, Navy, Air Force, and Marines. It also has the right to declare war. But in modern times, the United States entered the Korean War and Vietnam War at a president's direction without formal approval from Congress.

Congress has many other responsibilities. It controls the post offices, helps to build roads, and decides on granting statehood—as it did with Alaska and Hawaii, the 49th and 50th states.

The Constitution separates some of the powers of the House of Representatives from those of the Senate. The House, for example, has the exclusive right to introduce all tax bills. The power to tax is one of its most important functions.

The Structure and Powers of Congress

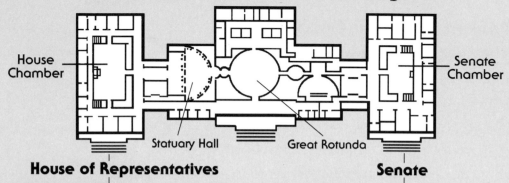

House Chamber

Senate Chamber

Statuary Hall

Great Rotunda

House of Representatives

- Made up of 435 Congress members— apportioned to each state according to population.

- Representatives must be at least 25 years old and must have been American citizens for at least 7 years.

- State apportionment of representatives changes every ten years, reflecting population data supplied by the census.

- House members are elected every two years.

- The leader of the majority party serves as the Speaker of the House. The Speaker controls debate in the House, has an important role in the selection of committee members and chairpersons, and can influence the scheduling and dispensation of legislation.

- Committees are organized by governmental areas (agriculture, defense, housing, etc.) to debate issues and formulate legislation.

- The House has 22 permanent committees, with more than 260 subcommittees.

- The House employs about 7,500 support staff members, plus additional members for committees.

Senate

- Made up of 100 senators—2 from each state.

- Senators must be at least 30 years old and must have been American citizens for at least 9 years.

- Senators are elected every 6 years. One-third are elected every two years.

- The leader of the majority party does not serve a prominent or important role. The vice-president is the leader of the Senate *pro-tempore,* meaning he or she may preside over the body if he or she wishes.

- Committees are organized by governmental areas (agriculture, defense, housing, etc.) to debate issues and formulate legislation.

- The Senate has 17 permanent committees, with more than 80 subcommittees.

- The Senate employs about 3,600 support staff members plus additional members for committees.

Together more than 23,000 staff employees work for Congress.

The House also has the power to begin the impeachment process against a president. To impeach means to charge an official with a crime. The House begins the process, but the Senate tries the president. If a president commits treason or breaks a serious law, impeachment gives the people the right to punish the president and to remove him or her from office. Impeachment proceedings have taken place only twice in the history of the United States: once against Andrew Johnson in 1868, and again against President Richard Nixon in 1974. Johnson was spared from impeachment by one vote. Nixon resigned before a vote could be taken.

In a presidential election, if there is no majority winner, the House decides who is president. Twice in our history—in the election of 1800, when Thomas Jefferson was elected, and in that of 1824, when John Quincy Adams became president—the House took the final vote. The candidate who received the most votes became president.

The Senate also serves as a check and balance to the power of the president. The Senate must agree to the appointment of the people the president selects for certain positions. All ambassadors, justices of the Supreme Court, judges of lower federal courts, cabinet members, some members of independent agencies, and senior military officers must receive senatorial approval. Congress's approval process ensures that people in power will serve the nation and not themselves.

Richard Nixon resigned his presidency in 1974, after the Congress voted to begin impeachment proceedings against him.

The Members

of Congress

America's Founders considered the House of Representatives to be the part of the federal government that is closest to the people of the United States. The 435 congressional members elected to the House, as it is often called, are elected by the people in their districts for two-year terms. The population of each state determines the number of its representatives. In 1990, California was the largest state, with 47 representatives. Several states have only one representative, including Delaware, Wyoming, Montana, and Alaska. Every ten years a census, a count of the population of each state, determines the number of representatives each state may have.

Opposite: The 435 members of the House of Representatives meet in their chamber inside the Capitol Building.

Unlike the House, where the larger states have more representatives (and because of their larger numbers quite possibly more power), in the Senate all states are equal. Each state, regardless of its population, elects two senators.

Qualifications of Congress Members

Anyone elected to the Senate must be at least 30 years of age, have been a citizen for at least 9 years, and live in the state from which he or she is elected. (The writers of the Constitution thought people's interests would be better served if all citizens were represented by someone local.)

To run for the House, a person must be at least 25 years of age, have been a citizen for 7 years, and reside in the state where he or she is elected.

Senators and representatives can come from all walks of life. Many senators, for example, formerly practiced law. But the Senate also includes one or more former newspaper publishers, bankers, tax accountants, journalists, restaurant owners, real estate brokers, political science professors, farmers, business executives, and social workers. One senator was formerly a professional basketball player and one was an astronaut.

Terms of Office

Senators are elected for six years, whereas U.S. representatives serve two-year terms of office. The

Founders intended that the Senate would spend a

longer time on issues than the House and that it would consider long-term goals. The six-year term gives senators more security in their positions. Ideally, it also allows them to remain more objective because they do not have to worry about pleasing the voters every two years.

Running for Congress

As the Constitution originally provided, America's senators were not directly elected by the people. Originally, they were chosen by state legislatures. An amendment to the Constitution changed that, and now senators as well as representatives are elected by public vote.

Members of both houses are chosen in state elections held in the November of every even-numbered year. Most states also hold primaries, or preliminary elections, several months before the general elections. In the congressional primaries, the Democrats and the Republicans—the two major parties—hold public elections to choose their candidates for the general election.

One-third of the Senate is up for reelection every two years. How can this be when senators serve six-year terms? The first Congress, convened in 1789, realized that a completely new Senate every six years would be a disadvantage. All of the senators would be inexperienced. None would have heard the discussions of bills and issues that occurred during the previous six years.

Congress members devote much of their time to campaigning for reelection. Here, Iowa Senator Tom Harkins meets voters during a campaign stop.

The first Senate drew lots to create an original membership of three groups—those who would serve two, four, and six years. Since then, all senators have been elected for six years, but their terms end in different years. This way, there is always a group of senior senators to guide junior senators.

Each person running for Congress organizes an election or reelection campaign. He or she will have a campaign manager; an advertising coordinator, who will be responsible for television and radio commercials; a media expert who will manage a candidate's press conferences, interviews, and public appearances; a speechwriter; and campaign workers.

Political Parties

The Constitution does not mention political parties. Yet today, most voting Americans and their elected officials belong to one of the two major parties: the Republicans or the Democrats.

When the Constitution was written, two groups, one called the Federalists and the other the Anti-Federalists, dominated. The Federalists favored the Constitution, but the Anti-Federalists did not.

The Democratic party arose in the 1820s and 1830s. Andrew Jackson is given credit for starting it. The Republican party officially began in 1854 as a movement of people dedicated to stopping slavery.

Since 1933, the Democrats have been the dominant party in Congress. Republicans have

The party in power, either Democrat or Republican, often uses a technique called *gerrymandering* to increase its chances of winning a congressional contest. Voting patterns have demonstrated over the years that some districts nearly always vote either Democratic or Republican. The party in power can change the boundaries of a district so that more of its members will be living in that area.

Gerrymandering started in 1812, when an election district in Massachusetts was changed in order to favor the so-called Democratic-Republican party of Governor Elbridge Gerry and hurt the chances of the Federalist party to win the election. The term *gerrymandering* comes from Governor Gerry's name.

Since 1964, it has been more difficult for politicians to gerrymander a district in favor of their party. In that year the Supreme Court ruled that each district should be equal in population. However, despite the federal court decision, gerrymandering continues. District boundaries may be redrawn so that all the Republican voters, for example, are grouped in the same district, even though the district is the same size as all the others.

controlled Congress for only two years since 1933. But despite the fact that Democrats hold an edge in registered voters, Republicans have won every presidential campaign since 1976. Jimmy Carter, a Democrat, won in 1976. But Republican Ronald Reagan won in 1980 and 1984, and Republican George Bush was voted president in 1988.

It is difficult to state exactly how the Democrats and the Republicans differ. For the most part, the Democrats have been the party of wage earners, union members, and minority groups. Republicans have been favored more by businesspeople and by those who believe in individual enterprise rather than in government action.

HOW A BILL INTRODUCED IN THE HOUSE OF REPRESENTATIVES BECOMES A LAW

(A similar procedure is followed for bills introduced in the Senate)

HOW BILLS ORIGINATE

The executive branch inspires much legislation. The president usually outlines broad objectives in the yearly State of the Union address.

Members of the president's staff may draft bills and ask Congress members who are friendly to the legislation to introduce them.

Other bills originate independently of the administration, perhaps to fulfill a campaign pledge made by a Congress member.

HOW BILLS ARE INTRODUCED

Each bill must be introduced by a member of the House. The speaker then assigns the bill to the appropriate committee.

The committee conducts hearings during which members of the administration and others may testify for or against the bill.

If the committee votes to proceed, the bill goes to the Rules Committee, which decides whether to place it before the House.

THE HOUSE VOTES

A bill submitted to the House is voted on, with or without a debate. If a majority approves it, the bill is sent to the Senate.

SENATE PROCEDURE

The Senate assigns the bill to a Senate Committee, which holds hearings and then approves, rejects, rewrites, or shelves the bill.

If the committee votes to proceed, it is submitted to the Senate for a vote, which may be taken with or without a debate.

RESULTS

If the Senate does not change the House version of the bill, and a majority approves it, the bill goes to the president for signing.

If the bill the Senate approves differs from the House version, the bill is sent to a House-Senate conference for a compromise solution.

If the conference produces a compromise bill, and it is approved by both the House and Senate, the bill goes to the president for signing.

WHEN A BILL BECOMES LAW

The bill becomes law if the president signs it. If the president vetoes it, two-thirds of both the House and Senate must approve it again before it can become law. If the bill comes to the president soon before Congress adjourns, the president may not do anything at all. If the bill is not signed before Congress adjourns, the bill dies. This is called the president's "pocket veto."

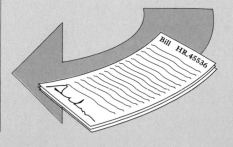

Congress

at Work

The principal work of Congress is passing laws, or legislation. In its first stages, a law is called a bill. During a typical congressional session, close to 10,000 new bills are introduced. No member of Congress could be familiar with so many bills. And as society becomes more complex, the bills often deal with technical matters that the members need to find out about. It is in special smaller committees that Congress discusses the bills and does most of the work on them.

The Committee System

The committees screen bills and eliminate those they find unnecessary. If a committee finds that it is

Opposite:
The main function of Congress is to propose, debate, and vote on the laws that govern the United States.

33

dealing with a lot of technical issues, it may create subcommittees to handle some of those issues.

The House of Representatives has 22 standing, or permanent, committees, and the Senate has 17. Among the committees are ones that deal with education, foreign relations, basic government operations, the postal service, the armed services, and budgets and appropriations. (Appropriations are the process of setting aside government funds for uses that Congress has approved.) Special committees are also formed when Congress wants to investigate something new or urgent.

The Progress of a Bill

All tax and appropriation bills must start in the House; any other bill can start in either the House or the Senate. For example, a senator may propose a bill to outlaw certain activities that add to air pollution if he or she believes that voters would favor such a measure. The senator meets with experts, drafts a bill, and formally submits it to the Senate. The Senate clerk gives the bill a name and a number, and it is assigned to a standing committee. Among the standing committees in the Senate are Foreign Relations; Environment and Public Works; Housing and Urban Affairs; and Agriculture, Nutrition, and Forestry.

Once a bill is in a committee, the committee may decide to hold hearings on the bill to obtain more information about it. At these hearings, which are open to the public, government officials, professors, or other experts in the field that the bill deals with provide information about the possible effects of the bill. With this added information, the committee may do one of three things:

• It may do nothing and "kill" the bill. The majority of bills "die" in committee.

• It may rewrite the bill.

• It may send the bill to the full House or Senate for a debate and vote.

If a majority of the voting members of the house where it began approve the bill, it goes to the other house, where it is assigned to a committee and discussed. Then, if the committee releases it, the bill is debated and voted on. If the other house does not approve the bill by a majority vote, it dies. Sometimes the other house adds changes, or amendments, to the original bill before approving it. It then goes to a joint committee, made up of members of both houses, where members try to iron out their differences. When they agree on a final version of the bill, both houses go ahead and cast a vote on it.

If both houses vote for a bill, it is sent to the president, who may do one of four things:

• Sign the bill, which then becomes a law.

• Veto, or formally reject, the bill. If the president vetoes it, Congress can override the veto by passing the bill again. But two-thirds of the members must vote for it.

35

• Do nothing. If Congress is still in session 10 days after the bill was sent to the president, and the president has neither signed it nor vetoed it, it becomes a law anyway.

• Use the so-called "pocket veto." If the president does nothing about the bill, and Congress adjourns before the 10 days are up, the bill dies. If Congress wants to pass the bill, it must reintroduce it in the next session and go through the process again.

Filibusters and Cloture

Because the Senate has only 100 members and is about one-fourth the size of the House, Senate debates of a bill can be more extensive. In the House, a member is expected to speak for no more than five minutes during debates. But senators can speak for as long as they wish. In fact, they sometimes use a stalling tactic called a "filibuster."

A filibuster is a prolonged speech in which a senator or group of senators tries to talk endlessly until the bill is killed. The goal is to tie up the bill for such a long period that it never comes to a vote. With other bills piling up, the majority leader (leader of the majority party) may have no choice but to send the delayed bill back to a committee, essentially killing it.

To continue a filibuster, a senator must simply talk, and talk, and talk about anything. In the past, senators have been known to discuss the Bible, Shakespeare, and baseball. One even read names

Serving as a member of Congress involves much responsibility and pressure. Members of Congress receive many privileges and special benefits that are intended to help them perform their jobs. For example, Congress members receive free mailing privileges, which enable them to keep their constituents (people who live in their state or district) informed of what they are doing. They receive free prescription drugs, an allowance for their personal staff, discounted haircuts, free stationery, money to produce newsletters, free insurance, free legal counsel, and even free parking at airports. And they can dine in the exclusive congressional restaurant. Until recently, they could also make use of a private athletic gym for the modest sum of $100 per year. When the press put the spotlight on these privileges, Congress increased the fee for the gym to $100 per quarter. Members of Congress do not even have to wait on bank lines. They can use a special congressional bank that operates on the first floor of the U.S. Capitol building.

Congressional members can also use the special privilege of cashing a check for more than they have in their congressional bank accounts. In 1992, a scandal arose when the press learned that some members of Congress had written checks for more than existed in their accounts. An investigation revealed that 8,331 checks were overdrafts. Several members who had written over 200 bad checks each were forced to resign, decided not to run for reelection, or faced criticism from their voters.

Members of Congress have been criticized for accepting too many "free benefits." One investigative television show videotaped several members at the beach in Barbados, where they had gone at taxpayers' expense. In 1990, members of Congress accepted over 500 free trips that were paid for by various corporate or trade associations.

from the telephone book. When tired of talking for so long, a senator can call on a fellow senator to continue the discussion. Filibusters have lasted for days, weeks, and in certain cases, even months.

The way to end a filibuster is by *cloture*, whereby two-thirds of all senators vote to end the discussion.

37

Critics say that filibusters prevent the Senate from passing bills and going about its business. But others believe that filibusters give senators the right to present their views on a bill and to force a debate.

Lobbyists and Lobbying

When America's Founders wrote the Constitution in the late 1700s, they wanted Congress members to represent the people. But the world has changed in the 200 years since the Constitution was written. One critic of the way our government operates today said that, in the 1990s, "Congressmen do not represent the people, but rather special interests." Not everyone agrees with that view, but most people agree that special interest groups or lobbyists exercise considerable influence over many politicians.

Lobbyists, or lobby groups, represent many special interest groups across the United States and the world. Lobbyists or groups may represent a corporation or group of corporations, such as automobile companies, or a profession, such as banking or medicine or meatpackers. Special interest groups also include advocates of a cause or ideology, such as civil rights or environmental protection. There are also lobby groups for people who believe in allowing abortion and for those who want to prevent abortions, for gun control and against gun control, for milk and oil producers, labor groups, and retired people, to name a few.

Lobbyists try to make members of Congress aware of the concerns that special interest groups have. Here, Cuban lobbyist Alicia Torres, leaves the Capitol Building.

In order to conduct their activities, lobbyists must register with the federal government.

Groups can also influence the government by forming political action committees (PACs). PACs can help finance a politician's campaign with the hope that the politician will later support their interests when he or she is voted into office.

Notable Debates and

Acts of Congress

Did Congress in the 1820s have a right to forbid a state to enter the union because it permitted slavery? Should a president be dismissed for breaking laws? Should a judge's personal life be considered during confirmation for a Supreme Court appointment? These have been a few of the highly charged issues that Congress has faced.

The Missouri Compromise

In 1819, America was still split over the issue of slavery. Eleven states forbade slavery and eleven states permitted it. Then Missouri, a slave state, requested statehood because its population had passed the 60,000 minimum requirement.

Opposite:
After months of heated debate, Henry Clay helped the Northern and Southern states to reach a compromise on certain slavery restrictions in 1820.

41

The next year, Congress hotly debated the Constitution's view of slavery in new states and purchased territories. Could Congress indeed forbid slavery in new states? One representative argued that states had their own rights, and that Congress did not have power over states. Southerners argued that since slaves were considered property, the Fifth Amendment ensured the right of ownership.

Henry Clay, the speaker of the House, helped achieve a compromise. Under the Missouri Compromise in 1820, Missouri was allowed to enter the Union as a slave state, and Maine, once part of Massachusetts, came in as a free, or slaveless, state. A line drawn across the Louisiana Purchase marked the regions where new states would be "free" (north of it) or "slave" (south of the line). The Missouri Compromise earned Henry Clay the nickname "Great Compromiser."

★★★★★★ CONGRESSIONAL INVESTIGATIONS ★★★★★★

One of the most important powers that the Constitution grants the Congress is the power of investigation. If Congress thinks there is a national problem, it can authorize a special investigation into the possible causes. In fact, in 1912 Congress investigated why a select few people were making millions and millions of dollars. This special committee on the distribution of money interviewed people like J.P. Morgan, one of the wealthiest people in the country at the time.

Congress also has the right to investigate another branch or department of the government. For example, if Congress thinks the Federal Bureau of Investigation (FBI) or Central Intelligence Agency (CIA) is not living up to its mission, it can establish a committee, investigate the agency, and make recommendations.

The Civil Rights Bill of 1964

By the 1960s, America had come a long way from slavery, which had been abolished almost 100 years before. African Americans could now vote, and many held important jobs in the community. But serious discrimination against blacks, women, Hispanics, and many other minority groups still continued. These minority groups were excluded from jobs for no other reason than their race, sex, color, or creed. In 1964, President Lyndon B. Johnson asked Congress to take steps to end that discrimination.

Not everyone agreed with Johnson's Civil Rights Bill. Many senators and representatives felt that blacks and members of other minorities could improve their lives on their own if they only wanted to. After much debate, Congress passed the Civil Rights Act of 1964. The Civil Rights Act created the Equal Employment Opportunity Commission (EEOC). To this day, the commission dedicates itself to ensuring that no discrimination exists in the workplace, in housing, or in any area of American society. The commission also tries to resolve discrimination cases on its own, but must go to the courts to prevent discrimination.

During the civil rights movement of the 1960s, Americans demanded equality for African Americans and other minorities.

The Watergate Hearings

The Watergate hearings in 1973 demonstrated the power of the Senate to investigate a president's wrongdoings. In 1972, when Richard Nixon was running for reelection, five members of his re-election committee were arrested for breaking into the Democratic National Committee headquarters at the Watergate apartments. Despite the negative publicity, Nixon was reelected in 1972. But articles by two *Washington Post* journalists, Carl Bernstein and Bob Woodward, led to a Senate hearing.

In 1973, the Senate appointed a special select committee to investigate the Watergate scandal. It uncovered a number of illegal activities carried out by either the president or his advisers. President Nixon's chief of staff, attorney general, and other leading advisers resigned in the face of the evidence. Further investigation revealed that Nixon had attempted to cover up the burglary.

The House Judiciary Committee began the impeachment process. After lengthy discussion, the committee voted to recommend that the House impeach the president. Facing this action, President Nixon resigned from the presidency in 1974 before the hearings could begin. The investigation demonstrated once again that the system of checks and balances works, that Congress is able to investigate even the president, and that not even the president of the United States can break laws.

After a long, controversial round of hearings in 1987, Congress voted to reject the nomination of Robert Bork (center) to the Supreme Court.

The Bork and Thomas Hearings

The Constitution states that the Senate must approve major presidential appointees. Over the last few years controversy has erupted over several nominations to the Supreme Court.

In 1987, President Ronald Reagan appointed Robert H. Bork, a U.S. Court of Appeals judge, to the Supreme Court to replace Justice Lewis F. Powell. Bork was an extremely outspoken judge who had strong views on rights of privacy and other issues. Asked questions about his views on abortion, he refused to answer. Many senators did not trust his response. After much debate, the Senate rejected Robert Bork's nomination by a vote of 58–42. Judge Anthony Kennedy was later appointed and approved by the Senate.

In 1991, President Bush nominated Clarence Thomas to the Supreme Court. A former assistant of his, Professor Anita Hill, accused Thomas of sexual harassment. She stated that he had used his position to ask her out on dates. Such actions are illegal because of Title VII of the Civil Rights Act of 1984, which forbids employers to make sexual advances toward their staff. Thomas denied all of the charges. The Senate Judiciary Committee publicly heard both testimonies. Who was telling the truth? In the end, the Senate Judiciary Committee believed Clarence Thomas. He was approved by the Senate and became a member of the U.S. Supreme Court.

In 1991, Senate confirmation hearings for Judge Clarence Thomas quickly catapulted the issue of sexual harassment into America's national news spotlight. Anita Hill testified that Thomas had harrassed her while the two worked together in Washington.

Glossary

amendment   A revision made to a bill, law, or the Constitution.

anarchy   Mob rule; absence of a government.

appropriations   Money set aside by Congress for specific uses.

aristocracy   Landowners; members of a wealthy class.

boycott   Refusal to use or purchase certain goods in protest.

civil rights   Those rights guaranteed to all individuals by the Thirteenth, Fourteenth, Fifteenth, and Nineteenth amendments of the Constitution. For example, the right to vote.

cloture   A vote to end a filibuster.

compromise   A settlement in which each side makes concessions.

filibuster   A tactic used by senators to stall a vote.

gerrymandering   Redistricting voting areas to increase a political party's chances of winning an election.

impeachment   Charging a political official with a crime.

militia   Military force made up of troops who are not members of the regular armed forces, but who are called to fight in an emergency.

monarch   King or queen.

political action committee (PAC)   Special interest group that bands together to influence politicians by helping to finance campaigns.

primaries   Preliminary elections.

tyranny   Too much power by a ruler or government.

veto   Rejection of a bill; usually by the president.

For Further Reading

Green, C. and Sanford, W. *The Congress.* Vero Beach, FL: Rourke, 1989.

Johnson, Linda Carlson. *Our Constitution.* Brookfield, CT: The Millbrook Press, 1992.

Schleifer, Jay. *Our Declaration of Independence.* Brookfield, CT: The Millbrook Press, 1992.

Schlesinger, Arthur M., ed. *The Federal Government: How It Works.* Broomall, PA: Chelsea House, 1990.

Stein, R.C. *The Powers of Congress.* Chicago: Childrens Press, 1989.

Index

Index